FASTBACK® Horror

Tomb of Horror

JANET LORIMER

GLOBE FEARON
Pearson Learning Group

FASTBACK® HORROR BOOKS

The Caller	The MD's Mistake
The Disappearing Man	Night Games
The Hearse	Night Ride
Live Bait	No Power on Earth
The Lonely One	The Rare Shell
The Masterpiece	**Tomb of Horror**

Cover Rubberball Productions/Getty Images, Inc. All photography © Pearson Education, Inc. (PEI) unless specifically noted.

Copyright © 2004 by Pearson Education, Inc., publishing as Globe Fearon®, an imprint of Pearson Learning Group, 299 Jefferson Road, Parsippany, NJ 07054. All rights reserved. No part of this book may be reproduced or transmitted in any form or by any means, electronic or mechanical, including photocopying, recording, or by any information storage and retrieval system, without permission in writing from the publisher. For information regarding permission(s), write to Rights and Permissions Department.

Globe Fearon® and Fastback® are registered trademarks of Globe Fearon, Inc.

ISBN 0-13-024522-4
Printed in the United States of America
1 2 3 4 5 6 7 8 9 10   07 06 05 04 03

1-800-321-3106
www.pearsonlearning.com

Toni glanced at her watch. It was only ten o'clock. With any luck, she and Randy would be setting up camp before noon. She grinned as she imagined how their afternoon would be spent. She'd probably be the one to do most of the work because her brother was too eager to start digging in that old mine.

She stretched, enjoying the hot sun on her back. What a perfect week to go camping. Springtime in the mountains. A whole week away from her classes at the university. Toni was really looking forward to a vacation from classes, homework and tests. Randy needed a vacation, too. He was working much too hard at his job as a geologist.

Randy staggered out of the store, his arms full of groceries. "Hey, sis, help me with this stuff."

Toni grabbed a bag that was about to tear. "What did you do, buy the whole store?" she laughed.

"Just making sure we have enough supplies," he said. "Once we locate that mine, I don't want to have to leave till the end of the week."

The elderly storekeeper appeared, carrying the last bag. "Did you say you're looking for a mine?"

"The Kroeger mine," Randy said. "I came across the records a couple of weeks ago. Has anyone ever tried to find it?"

The old man shook his head. "That mine's not lost, mister. Everyone around here knows where it is. But no one wants to go near it! If you're smart, you'll stay away, too."

"Why?" Randy asked.

The old man looked uneasy. "It's a bad place. Dangerous. Kroeger found that mine back during the gold rush. There was an accident. The main tunnel caved in. A lot of men died. Since then, folks leave it alone."

"I can understand that," Randy said. "Abandoned mines can be very dangerous. But I'm a geologist. I know what I'm doing." He started to get into the jeep.

"Wait a minute!" the storekeeper said. He sounded upset and Toni thought she saw fear in his eyes. "You don't understand! I'm not talking about that kind of danger. I'm talking about . . ." He paused, biting his lower lip nervously.

"Go on," Toni said.

"You'll probably think I'm crazy," said the old man, "but I'm going to tell you anyway. That mine is cursed."

"Cursed!" Randy hooted with laughter. "You've got to be kidding!"

"Go ahead and laugh," snapped the old man. His face turned red with anger. "But it's true! Only a fool would go up to that mine!" He started back to the store.

"Wait!" Toni cried. "Why do you say it's cursed?"

The old man turned around, glaring at her. "I'm not saying another word, lady. I'm just warning you! Stay away from that place!"

"Come on, Toni," Randy said, grabbing her arm. "Let's get out of here."

Toni shook her brother's hand off. "I wanted to hear what he had to say," she said, angrily. "You shouldn't have made fun of him, Randy."

"He probably wants to keep the mine for himself," Randy said. "It must be richer than I thought. I'm not stupid enough to buy that talk about ghosts."

"He didn't say it was haunted," Toni said. "He said it was cursed."

"Cursed, haunted—what's the difference? Let's talk about something else."

"You never told me how you found out about the mine," Toni said.

"Look at this." Her brother pulled an old leather bound book from his pocket. "It's Kroeger's journal. I found it in a second hand bookstore a couple of months ago. There's a map of the mine's location in the book. I started to dig back through the records and sure enough, I found the date that Kroeger had registered the claim."

"What happened to him after the cave-in?"

"It was a bad one," Randy said. "Everyone but Kroeger was trapped in the mine. I guess it was too much for him. He went insane and died six months later."

Toni shivered. "Poor man! What else does the journal say?"

"Oh, I didn't get that from the journal. It's all in German. I found out about the accident and Kroeger from some old news clippings."

"All in German?" Toni said. She couldn't help grinning. "Is that why you wanted me to come along? So I could translate this journal for you? It's nice having a sister who's majoring in foreign languages, isn't it?"

Randy laughed. "No. I don't need you to read the journal. In fact, I bet it's pretty dull. All I needed was the map."

Toni thumbed through the yellowed pages, trying to read the faded handwriting. Randy might find it dull, but she was curious. Near the end, she read something that made her frown. Kroeger's last entry had been written in a hurry. The handwriting was almost a scrawl. But Toni caught the German word *verboten*—forbidden! And, she couldn't forget the look of fear in the storekeeper's eyes. She made up her mind to read the journal as soon as they set up camp.

Several hours later Randy pulled the jeep off the road into a small meadow. From this point they would hike the rest of the way.

It was late afternoon when Randy stopped walking and pointed through the trees. "That looks like a building."

"Is it the mine?" Toni asked.

"It's around here, according to the map. Let's take a look."

They pushed through the trees, coming at last to a small clearing. On the opposite side was a small wooden shack. Beyond it, a few hundred yards up a trail, was what looked like the entrance to a mine tunnel.

"This is it!" Randy said excitedly.

"It sure is quiet up here," Toni said. Suddenly she felt uneasy.

"I'm going to look at the mine," Randy said. "You stay here till I know it's safe."

"Be careful," Toni warned. She watched him walk away, and felt her uneasiness growing. It was still afternoon but for some reason this spot seemed very gloomy. Toni shivered, pulling the collar of her jacket higher around her neck. The temperature here seemed much lower than it had been on the trail they'd just climbed. Toni looked around at the thick pines which were all around the clearing. They shut out most of the light. For a moment longer she stood still, listening. There were no sounds, not even birds singing or squirrels chattering.

Toni shivered again. Maybe a storm was coming. She'd better get to work, setting up their camp. Then she took another look at the cabin. It looked sturdy enough, and if there was a storm on the way, it might provide them with shelter. She decided to check it out.

Although it was very old, it still seemed

to be in good condition. Toni pushed the door open and then peered into the darkness. A few thin shafts of light slipped through some cracks in the wooden roof and fell across a dirt floor. A stone fireplace had been built into one wall. The air inside seemed warm and had a musty odor. Toni stepped inside.

The roof was strong enough, she saw, and the fireplace looked useable. Strangely, there were no signs of animal life in the cabin. No spiderwebs, no mouse nests, no small tracks on the floor. It was almost as if, from the moment Kroeger left this place, time had stood still.

She stepped outside, wondering how Randy was doing. She saw him walking down the trail from the mine. He was carrying something.

"What did you find?" Toni called.

Randy looked at her with a puzzled expression. "That wasn't an accidental cave-in," he said. "The entrance to the mine was sealed on purpose.

"That doesn't make sense," Toni said.

"I know. Unless . . ." He held up the thing he had found. It was a rough, handmade wooden cross. "This was over the entrance. Kroeger must have put it there. He must have sealed up the mine after the cave-in. Maybe he thought of the mine as a tomb after his friends were killed."

"I don't like this place," Toni said. "Can't we camp someplace else and just forget about the mine?"

"No!" Randy snapped. "Look, Toni, I didn't come all this way to be spooked by that old storekeeper's nonsense. We're staying!" He broke the cross into pieces and threw them into the bushes. "Let's set up camp," he said, pushing past Toni. She followed him slowly, unable to shake off her growing nervousness.

Randy agreed that they should sleep in the cabin. While Toni started a fire, her brother unrolled their sleeping bags. They ate supper in near silence, each lost in thought. Now and then Toni glanced through the open door. The sun was setting behind the tall mountain peaks and long shadows, like dark fingers, reached across the clearing.

Randy suddenly tossed his empty plate aside. He grabbed a pick and shovel and one of the gas lanterns.

"Where are you going?" Toni cried in alarm.

"Up to the mine. I want to start breaking some of those rocks loose at the entrance."

"Randy, wait! It's almost dark! Can't you do it in the morning?"

"We've only got a week," he said. "I'll need every minute of light."

Suddenly Toni saw the look in her brother's eyes. Gold fever! She should have guessed that this was more than a vacation for Randy.

He slammed the door shut behind him, leaving Toni with a feeling of despair. She huddled closer to the fire, more for comfort than for warmth.

Then she remembered the journal. Reading that would at least give her something to do. And maybe it would keep her from feeling depressed.

At first it was hard to read the faded handwriting. But soon Toni found herself caught up in Kroeger's story. Kroeger had sailed from Germany to California in 1850. On the ship he met people from many other countries. They were all heading for the gold fields in the hopes of striking it rich. One man, named Drayfuss, was a coffin maker. He was a strange, silent man who carried all his belongings in a coffin.

When the ship docked in San Francisco, Drayfuss asked if he could travel with Kroeger and his companions. The other miners didn't want Drayfuss around. But Kroeger felt sorry for him. He talked the others into letting Drayfuss join their party.

Toni threw more wood on the fire. Kroeger's story was getting interesting.

A few weeks after they left San Francisco, they discovered a rich vein of gold high in the mountains. The miners were excited, certain that this mine would make them rich!

Then disaster struck! One morning they found several of the mules dead. Their throats had been ripped open and all the blood had been drained from their bodies.

Toni shuddered, but she couldn't stop reading.

The men decided a bear must have killed the mules. That night they posted a guard, but in the morning they discovered that the man had mysteriously disappeared. The miners stopped working in the mine and formed a search party. But they found no sign of their missing companion. That night they posted more men to guard the camp. By the next morning, these men had also disappeared.

A log collapsed in the fire, sending up a shower of sparks. Toni jumped at the sudden noise. She glanced over her shoulder. The firelight couldn't break through the thick shadows that coiled in the corners of the room. She strained to listen for some sound to tell her Randy was returning. But all she heard was the clang of his pick against the rocks. With a sigh, she went back to the journal.

The miners were determined to trap and kill the bear. They strengthened the corral and at night they posted more guards. Fires were built to keep wild animals away.

Kroeger stood guard until he was relieved shortly before midnight. Exhausted he climbed into his bedroll and fell into a sound sleep. He awoke just as the sun was coming up to find the cabin deserted. He heard faint hoofbeats in the distance. Kroeger ran outside just in time to see Drayfuss disappearing down the trail. He ran to the corral. A horrible sight met his eyes. The rest of the mules were dead and none of his companions were anywhere to be found.

Kroeger searched the woods around the camp, repeatedly calling his friends' names. But the only sound he heard was that of his own voice echoing back to him. When he returned to the campsite he found it was still deserted. Kroeger was utterly baffled. How could the men have disappeared so silently, without leaving a trace? And why?

Then Kroeger remembered the mine. Was it possible that his companions could be there? He had no idea what he might find, but he was determined to search the entire network of tunnels. He took a lantern and entered the main tunnel.

Toni glanced at her watch. It was very late. What was keeping Randy? Was he going to work at the mine all night?

She went to the door and opened it, peering into the darkness. It was pitch black. There was no sound but the wind moaning through the pines.

"Randy?" she called.

No answer. She waited, then called his name again. Still no answer. The silence folded itself around her like a black cloak.

Toni closed the door, and this time she bolted it. She went back to the fire and threw the rest of the wood on the flames. The fire crackled merrily, but its light and warmth could not erase her worry.

She picked up the journal and continued to read.

At the end of one tunnel, Kroeger rounded a turn and saw, in the dim light, a horrible sight. The bodies of his companions were spread all over the floor. The air was thick with the smell of rotting meat.

The faces of the dead men were a terrible grayish color. Splatters of dried blood crusted their skin and clothing. Leaning over, Kroeger realized that they, like the mules, had been drained of all their blood.

As he stared in shock at the bodies, an icy chill went up his spine. He had the strange feeling that someone—or something—was watching him! He whirled about and saw glowing red eyes in the darkness. Kroeger was paralyzed with terror as a horrible creature moved toward him out of the shadows.

It was a man, but not a man. Its skin was the color of a dead man's, but the eyes glowed with inhuman life. Its clothing was rotted with the dampness of the grave. Kroeger screamed as the thing threw back its head and opened its mouth revealing sharp fangs.

Now he knew what had killed his companions and the mules. He knew why Drayfuss had run away. Drayfuss, servant to an unspeakable dark force, had brought this monster to America. He had turned this thing loose on an unsuspecting world.

Kroeger stepped backwards as the creature moved toward him. A noise behind him made him glance quickly over his shoulder. The figures on the ground were moving, rising to their feet. They lurched toward him, their eyes shining red, their hungry mouths open.

Kroeger threw his lantern at the creature that was blocking his path. Glass shattered, spilling flaming kerosene on the ground. The monster hissed, and moved back. The others stumbled backward into the tunnel, seeking the protection of the darkness. In that instant, Kroeger fled!

He barely escaped from the maze of tunnels. The creatures could not follow him into the sunlight. Kroeger sealed the entrance to the mine, hoping to bury them forever. The mine that had represented a dream of riches had become a tomb of horror.

Toni stared at the journal in terror. No wonder the storekeeper hadn't wanted to talk about the curse! Who would believe such a bizarre tale?

Kroeger's last entry screamed a final warning! "Do not remove the cross! It is the shield that guards this cursed tomb! If the cross is removed, mankind will be plunged into a nightmare of evil. Do not remove the cross! That is forbidden!"

The cross! Randy had taken it away from the entrance to the mine. Randy was opening the tomb! Oh, God, he had no idea what he was setting free . . .

Toni ran to the door, fumbling with the bolt.

At that instant, she heard a high-pitched scream in the distance.

"Randy!" she cried.

There was no answer. The silence closed in again. Toni clung to the door frame, peering into the darkness. Where was he? What had happened to him?

Fear gripped her. She slammed the door

and locked it, clinging to the wood for support.

She tried to tell herself that Randy might have had an accident. A rock could have fallen on him. He might be lying out there, bleeding and unconscious.

She gnawed her lower lip, wondering what to do. Should she believe Kroeger's story? Or had he created the awful tale out of his own sick mind?

Glancing around, Toni saw the second lantern. She hurried to light it. Waiting here was unbearable. She had to find out what had happened to Randy.

She picked up the lantern and walked slowly to the door. She tried to work up her courage to leave the safety of the cabin.

Then she heard a voice!

"Toni . . ."

It was Randy's voice. He was all right! With a happy cry, she put down the lantern and fumbled with the bolt.

The door swung slowly inward, the creaking of the hinges grating on the silence.

Then, without warning, the door crashed against the wall. Toni screamed! Standing on the threshold was Randy. But it was not the man she knew!

A hideous creature with her brother's features loomed over her. Reddened eyes gazed hungrily into hers. Grey lips were drawn back in a twisted grin, revealing sharp long fangs.

The monster raised its arms and lunged toward her. Toni staggered backward, screaming with terror. Her foot bumped against something and she lost her balance. She fell to the floor. The creature moved closer.

Out of the corner of her eye, she saw what she had tripped over. It was the gas lantern. Toni grabbed it and thrust it into the face of the thing that hovered over her.

The creature backed away, hissing as the heat and light touched it. Toni scrambled to her feet, ramming the lantern against cold, grey flesh, pushing the monster back into the night. It screamed with pain and staggered through the doorway. She slammed and bolted the door in one quick movement.

The creature pounded on the door in rage. Weeping now, Toni shrank back toward the fireplace.

The banging on the door became louder and stronger. There were more of those *things* out there. The creatures from the mine! They were all around the cabin now. Mindless, soulless creatures that hungered for her blood.

Toni looked at the hinges on the door. As she watched, a few splinters of wood broke free and fell to the ground. The door would not hold together much longer. The stack of firewood was gone. Soon there would be nothing but embers in the fireplace. The lantern would dim and die when its fuel was used up.

In a few hours, darkness would surround her. And then . . .

Toni backed as close to the fire as she could. She crouched down, curling her body into a tight little ball, whimpering.

Against the sound of the harsh blows striking the cabin, her voice, now oddly childish, could barely be heard.

"Don't turn out the light, Mommy! I'm scared of the dark . . ."